Joseph Henry Walker

A few facts and suggestions on money, trade and banking

Joseph Henry Walker

A few facts and suggestions on money, trade and banking

ISBN/EAN: 9783744739467

Printed in Europe, USA, Canada, Australia, Japan

Cover: Foto ©Lupo / pixelio.de

More available books at **www.hansebooks.com**

A FEW

FACTS AND SUGGESTIONS

ON

MONEY, TRADE, AND BANKING.

BY

J. H. WALKER.

BOSTON:
HOUGHTON, MIFFLIN AND COMPANY.
NEW YORK: 11 EAST SEVENTEENTH STREET.
The Riverside Press, Cambridge.
1882.

Copyright, 1881,
By HOUGHTON, MIFFLIN & CO.

All rights reserved.

The Riverside Press, Cambridge:
Stereotyped and Printed by H. O. Houghton and Company.

CONTENTS.

	PAGE
INTRODUCTION	5

CHAPTER I.
MONEY 7

CHAPTER II.
TRADE 15

CHAPTER III.
FUNCTION OF COIN 19

CHAPTER IV.
CAPITAL 22

CHAPTER V.
BORROWER AND LENDER 25

CHAPTER VI.
INTEREST 29

CHAPTER VII.
BANKING NECESSARY 33

CHAPTER VIII.
GOVERNMENT BONDS 35

CHAPTER IX.
NATIONAL BANKS 38

CHAPTER X.
BANKS IN THE INTEREST OF THE PEOPLE 44

CHAPTER XI.
INDUCEMENT TO ENGAGE IN BANKING 52

CHAPTER XII.
PRACTICAL WORKING OF A BANK 55

CHAPTER XIII.
THE CLEARING HOUSE 58

CHAPTER XIV.
BY WHOM MONEY IS MADE 62

CHAPTER XV.
IMPOTENCE OF STATUTE LAW 66

CHAPTER XVI.
CONCLUSION 71
   Government Legal Tender Notes 77
   U. S. Sub-treasury 81
   Legislation needed 87

APPENDIX.
SUMMARY OF THE PRINCIPAL RESTRICTIONS AND REQUIREMENTS OF THE NATIONAL BANK ACT 93

INTRODUCTION.

EVERY man in the community has now the same liberty to make and issue money, that he has to buy, sell, walk, run, lift, or do a dozen other things, — no law hindering him. The only restriction is, that his money shall not be made in imitation of that made by any other man.

Two to three hundred millions of dollars, in money, are made each day, doing the work of money for the day, and are destroyed at night.

Money is coin, or any non-interest bearing title to property, that can be immediately realized on, with the option of coin.

In what is herein presented, the endeavor is to make plain what MONEY, TRADE, and BANKING really are, spending no time on theories, and claiming to do nothing more than to present existing facts with reasonable clearness and free from all technicalities. There is no other department of knowledge in which theories are of so little value, — where experience should so exclusively be teacher and master. In finance, as in nearly all other things, the truth lies on the surface. If it has been missed it is because we have ploughed too deep for it. We have missed it because it was so near and so simple; we rejected it when we saw it. Furthermore, there is nothing in these questions that a plain man may not fully understand. In order to fairly cover the ground and make the statements reasonably complete, it will be necessary to state, formally, many familiar things.

MONEY, TRADE, AND BANKING.

CHAPTER I.

MONEY.

THE word MONEY conveys to the mind of the merchant the idea of everything in the shape of an obligation of one person or corporation upon another, which a bank will take for its face value. It is true that wage-workers and small farmers understand money to mean only coin and bank-notes; but only about two thousand millions of dollars are annually paid to wage-workers and small farmers, while thirty thousand millions of dollars of the annual exchanges of the property of the country, made by merchants and traders, are paid for with other forms of money. The farmer and wage-worker use the words MONEY or CASH to convey the idea of coin or bank-notes, because only coin and bank-notes do for them the work of money.

The meaning of the words *money* or *cash* to all others also includes everything that does the work of money, which besides coin and bank-notes are cashiers' checks, checks, drafts, bills of exchange, etc., each of which, excepting coin, are *titles to property*. The titles to property that annually change hands probably exceed seventy billions of dollars, to pass which scarcely three billions of dollars of currency and coin change hands.

Coins are pieces of gold or silver, stamped by the government for the purpose of indicating their weight and fineness, and for that purpose only. Stamping them adds, and can add, nothing to the purchasing power of gold or silver (excepting for brief periods and under exceptional conditions). This fact is very clearly stated in the law authorizing the issue of United States bonds and the redemption of the greenbacks, passed March 18, 1869, and July 14, 1870, which says, that they shall be paid "in coin or its equivalent of the (then) present standard value" (that is to say, coin of the same weight and fineness), which means so many pounds of gold [1] of a given fineness, precisely as we specify wheat of a given quality and number of bushels, in a contract for the delivery of wheat.

[1] All admit gold to be the standard of value; some claim that silver is equally so. As I do not wish to burden this discussion with any question of a double standard, each person may understand gold to include silver, or gold alone, according to his own opinion of what should constitute the standard of value. But in deciding the question we must remember that, in the light of reason and all the experience of the past, gold and silver cannot both be the standard of value at the same time, excepting for the brief period their lines of fluctuation in value cross each other. When a given weight of two metals is mentioned as the standard of value, the debtor class always fix on which it shall be, and invariably choose the cheaper one.

That the government coinage stamp adds nothing to the value, or purchasing power, of gold, is further shown by the fact that there is no merchant or banker who will not take gold, guaranteed to be of the same weight and fineness as $1,000 of gold coin, for $1,000 worth of property, as readily as the gold coin. Gold, having intrinsic value, is money, *and more:* it is property, capital; all other forms of money are titles to property. Of all the forms of money now used, gold only has the power in and of itself to pay debts, because it only is capital.

When coin passes from one person to another, actual property, or capital, passes, and the transaction is final in its nature; that is to say, there is no other thing to be done by the receiver in order to secure possession of actual property. By the transfer of nothing else, short of the passage of the final papers changing absolutely the residence of the title of actual property (and giving possession of the property) from one person to another, is the transaction final. There are many forms of transfers of titles[1] to property in common use, all of

[1] The word *claim*, as commonly used, conveys the idea of a disputed title to property. A *title* is commonly understood to mean a paper which securely vests the property in its holder, — an admitted title. A check, bill of exchange, etc., is either a *claim* upon the property of the maker (or indorser) for the amount named therein, or it is a *title* to so much of his property. Perhaps to call any one of them a *claim* would be more accurate as a legal term; but the universal and unvarying practice of business men to surrender promptly, to the holder, the amount of property named in any one of them, justifies the use of the word *title*, because it more accurately describes the thing.

which do the work of money and are counted in commercial transactions and accounts as CASH or MONEY, as before stated, each of which is indispensable in its place.

The titles to property, which are money, are: —

First. Bank-notes, which are forms of transfers of the property of banks, and are necessary to the affairs of every-day life. They require no act on the part of any one who uses them to make them complete. They are as readily received from strangers as acquaintances. They are, in essence, the checks, drafts, bills of exchange, etc., of all the men whose business is not large enough to require the direct assistance of the banker, and they are nothing more. They are for use in transactions so small that the other forms of money are not practicable or desirable. They are nearly identical in form, and perfectly identical in substance, with checks, drafts, etc., a more convenient form, for the persons using them, of the same thing. The law of the land recognizes no more value or power in them than in any ordinary demand note of one individual against another. No one can compel another to accept them in liquidation of a debt, any more than he can the demand note of an individual. They are the same in form and substance as an ordinary demand note, excepting that they are made payable to any one in possession of them, instead of to the order of some individual named in them. The law recognizes the power of nothing to discharge a debt, excepting a specified kind of property, and of the amount named in the paper acknowledging the debt. The law says the term "dollar" shall mean a given weight and fineness of gold. In fact, custom, or rather a universal law, as certain as any law of nature and recognized and acted upon as such the world over, has fixed the conditions of payment of any and every debt to be the transfer of a given weight and fineness of gold or silver. There is no exception anywhere, either among civilized or barbarous peoples. If any man accepts anything other than gold or silver, it is by his free consent, aside from the agreement made at the time the debt was contracted. This is the universal law and the universal custom.

Second. Cashiers' checks, which transfer, by the bank itself, the title to the property of the bank, to the amount named in the check, to the person or corporation named therein.

Third. Checks, which transfer the title of the individual making them, to the amount of property named therein, which he owns, that is in the possession of the bank upon which the check is made, to the person or corporation named in the check.

Fourth. Drafts, which are means of transferring the title of property from one individual or corporation to another, through the assistance of a bank.

Fifth. Bills of exchange, which transfer the title to the property of a banker in one country to an individual or banker in another country.

Accepting the declaration that "money is what money does" (which is the only practical definition of money), these five forms, by which the titles to property are exchanged, are preëminently *money*. Coin is scarcely ever passed, and bank-notes but seldom.

With these five simple forms of money are all the exchanges of the ownership of property between individuals and corporations made throughout the world, — exchanges so vast in the aggregate that they are beyond the comprehension of man. These forms of money are so simple that any school-boy can make them. They are as simple as the alphabet. They are the alphabet, or rather the language, of trade and commerce everywhere. They are as necessary and as indestructible as ordinary human language. They are as necessary to the vast exchanges of the world as are the canals, the steamboats, and the railways. They have grown up with, and are a part of, the means of making the actual exchanges of the products of the world. They are the concrete forms of the unwritten laws of trade, — laws as inexorable as are any of the laws of nature. They are as surely the result of ages of abrasion and accumulation as is the soil upon which we tread. Their money function has grown up with civilization, and in all matters pertaining to finance they are the exponent and vehicle of civilization. They are as independent of national boundaries and legislation as is international law.

Of the six enumerated forms of money, as has been before stated, coin is the only one that can do more than to transfer the title to property from one person to another. Not one of the others can extinguish debt. Notwithstanding this fact the universal practice is for each man to take, in exchange for his property, some one of these titles to the property of some other man. Every man takes all the titles to the property of every other man that he receives, and deposits them in a bank, and accepts in their place a title to the property of the bank, to an equal amount. This title to the property of the bank is always transferred by the individual having it to the same or some other bank in exchange for some title to his own property, which he has before given; and as each bank, the world over, sends all the money titles, or its equivalent, to the property it buys, not cancelled at its own counter, to the "clearing house," every money title issued ultimately finds its way there, and is there cancelled and destroyed, — meeting there the equivalent which each merchant is obliged to give some one, for each money title to his property which any one accepts from him. After any bank or clearing house has exhausted all the titles to the property of others which it has, in matching the titles it has issued, to its own property (which are presented to it), it must then give to every man who presents any further title to its property, gold to satisfy it. The fact that gold settles the *final balance* is equivalent to its being actually passed from one man to another in paying every debt in the country, to the exclusion of every other form of money, because the result is precisely the same as it would be if gold actually passed in each transaction. By this means it actually touches and measures the value of every commodity, in every trade, from the selling of a dozen of eggs to the funding of hundreds of millions of the public debt. Thus money grows out of trade, and is a part of it. It has no existence aside from it, and cannot be described without including trade.

CHAPTER II.

TRADE.

EVERY form of money, excepting coin, represents barter, and that only. Taking any other of the many forms of money is taking a title to the property of its maker to the value named in the bank-bill, cashier's check, check, draft, or bill of exchange, etc., as the case may be, in coin, and nothing more. In exchange for them, the person receiving them gives either a like amount of his property, or a title to it, or a title which he has to the property of some other person or banker. By means of these devices, primitive *barter* becomes modern trade, but is not changed in its substance. Each individual uses these devices to accurately divide and subdivide the unsecured title to his aggregate property into such portions as he wishes to exchange for the property of his neighbor. The crudest form of *barter* and modern trade are essentially the same. The only difference being in the number of persons who take part in a given transaction, the facility and accuracy with which property is divided and moved, and the accuracy with which values are computed. There can be no trade other than the exchanging of property for property, unless one person or class is content to maintain trade with another by exchanging something for nothing. The difference between the old and the new is development, not substitution. It is not abandoning the stage-coach and turnpike for the railway and railway cars. It is rather the development of the original loom into the loom that weaves the fancy cashmere of to-day. It is a loom still, retaining all its original features. The difference is in the devices for dividing the property of the purchaser into the exact amount that the party selling demands for the thing sold, — the number of persons uniting to do it, and the unanimous assent and assistance of all in consummating each transaction.

Besides the forms of exchangeable titles to the property of their makers and indorsers heretofore mentioned, namely: Bank-notes, cashiers' checks, checks, drafts, and bills of exchange, which by common consent are money, there are —

First. Individual and corporate titles to a specified amount of the property of their maker, called bankable notes, payable in the near future, at a time and place named therein.

Second. Individual or corporate titles to a specified amount of the property of their makers, called demand notes, payable on the demand of the party owning them.

Third. Book accounts, which in the country store represent primitive barter, in the settlement of which very little use is made of any of the devices for transferring titles to property, before described. The products of the farm or shop are directly exchanged for the goods of the trader.

Fourth. Stocks, each share of which is the title of the holder to that proportion of the whole property, described therein, which is owned by him.

Fifth. Bonds and mortgage notes of individuals or corporations secured by conditional bills of sale of certain specified property, described therein.

The passage of the title to a mortgage bond or note is always associated in our minds with the passage of the title to the property described in the mortgage; but, as a matter of fact, both in custom and law, the right of the owner of a mortgage bond or note to the property specified in the mortgage, is no more than is the right of the holder of any one of the other nine forms of titles to so much of the property of the maker thereof as will fully satisfy the obligation. The only difference is, that the owner of the mortgage bond or note has a prior right to the property mentioned in the mortgage. The holder of any of the other forms of obligation can levy on any kind or portion of the property of the maker not pledged by mortgage. To satisfy the owner of any one of the obligations the law requires the maker to deliver coin, and if the holder accepts any other form of money he simply exchanges his obligation against one party for an obligation against another party. Every one of the obligations named must, of necessity, represent property. The moment they cease to do that they are valueless. The theory and fact is, that each one of them specifies on its face the day on which the maker will deliver to the holder property of the value named therein, in the performance of which promise the obligation dies.

CHAPTER III.

FUNCTION OF COIN.

Coin, which is property and not an obligation, as are the other forms of money, is never passed, so long as the holder of an obligation desires or is willing to accept any form of capital other than coin; and as no income can be derived from coin, there is no inducement under ordinary circumstances for the creditor to demand it of the debtor, or for an individual receiving it to retain it in his possession. Nothing is properly called money which affords an income. It is fatal to the monetary function of an obligation to contain any inducement for an individual to keep it as an investment. Money is a title to property, from which no income is or can be derived, that can be immediately realized on, with the option of gold.

The only reason why banks hold, or should be required to hold any gold, is not because it is money, but because it is property, — property because of its intrinsic value, in and of itself, acknowledged as such the world over. The sphere of gold in the system of exchange is purely that of property used to settle the final balance, not of money, — understanding money to mean purely a circulating medium. Gold thereby becomes the measure of the value of every other kind of property. The monetary system of the civilized world treats gold as *the property* by which the value of all other property is measured. It measures it as gold *property*, not as money, and irrespective of the pieces into which it is divided, or the stamp they bear. We actually measure the value of any given thing by it, by determining how much weight of gold is demanded in exchange for the thing. Not by a process of reasoning, but by actually making the exchange. The ratio of that exchange fixes the price, in gold, of the thing exchanged for it, until another like exchange is made at a different ratio. This is accomplished by the banks. When the titles to the property of others, received by any bank on any day, are less in amount than the titles to its property which it is called upon to deliver to others, the difference is immediately settled by the delivery of coin.

The law requires coin to be passed in every transaction, and as long as the final balance is paid in coin, it is practically a perfect and literal compliance with the law. Coin measures the value of every article exchanged until the final exchange when coin itself passes in liquidation of a title, as truly as though it passed in every transaction; because the final result is precisely the same as though coin itself passed in each transaction. Thus it really and certainly measures all values. No one thinks of questioning the fact that the price at which the surplus of any particular brand of flour is sold in England for gold fixes its price in gold here. So with every other article a surplus of which is sold in Europe for gold. The millions worth of the same property exchanged here is every dollar of it exchanged on the basis of its gold value there. Gold as really measures the value of each thing exchanged as though it was passed by the buyer to the seller, for all the millions at which the whole is valued, every time a purchase is made.

So long as the banks are ready to pay gold to any one who has a title to any of their property, and demands gold in payment, and do actually pay it in settlement of the final balance against them, gold is practically present and does its office in every purchase and sale that is made in the land.

CHAPTER IV.

CAPITAL.

MANY terms in common use are technically far from accurate, and those of trade are no exception. We say the sun rises and sets, when we mean that the earth revolves. We say we wish we had more money, when we mean that we want more capital. We do not long for titles to capital, but for capital itself. Men very rarely borrow money, they borrow capital. A. has $50,000 in capital, all of which he uses himself, doing a business of $500,000 a year, but is at no time, for twenty-four hours, in actual possession of $100 in bank-bills or coin. B. has $100,000 in capital, $50,000 of which he uses himself, the other $50,000 he loans to his neighbors. When B. loans C. any of his capital, C. receives from B. a title to just that portion of the $50,000 which he borrows of B., say $10,000, and calls it money. C. immediately exchanges this $10,000 title to capital for $10,000 worth of any of the myriad forms of property he most desires to have. C. has parted with his *money*, but *he still has* exactly what he desired to have, and borrowed of B., namely, capital. B. has $10,000 less capital than before he loaned $10,000 to C., and has in its place a title to $10,000 of C.'s aggregate property. C.

has $10,000 more capital than before he borrowed of B. The papers that passed from B. to C., called money, were no more to the transaction than is the stick over the shoulder of the miner to the gold he carries on it, the jewel box to a lady's jewels, the basket used in gathering the crop, or the wagon that takes it to market, to the crop. They carry property, the piece or pieces of paper carried the capital that passed from B. to C.

While writing the above my eye fell upon the following newspaper paragraph :—

"The New York —— makes neat definitions : 'Mr. Longfellow can take a worthless sheet of paper, and by writing a poem on it make it worth $50. That's genius. Mr. Vanderbilt can take a sheet of paper, and by writing fewer words on it can make it worth $50,000,000. That's capital.'"

If this paragraph means anything, it means that the value of the worthless paper was made $50 by the creative power of Longfellow, and $50,000,000 by the creative power of Vanderbilt. That is to say, it declares that genius can, by its inherent power, add to the capital of the world the sum of $50, by making a worthless piece of paper worth $50, and a capitalist can, by his power as a capitalist, add $50,000,000 to the wealth of the world, by a few strokes of his pen upon a worthless piece of paper.

What Longfellow can do is to give us the results of a long life of application to his divine pursuit, in a poem that represents and is the result of labor, as much as gold dug from the mine, wheat raised upon the farm, useful things made from worthless wood, or beautiful vases from dull clay. The paper upon which it is written has no more connection with it than the spade of the gold-digger, the plough of the farmer, the tools of the wood-worker, or the wheel of the potter.

What Vanderbilt can do is to give to another a title to $50,000,000 — of his capital. When the person to whom it is given presents his title to, and takes possession of the $50,000,000 — of property, Vanderbilt has $50,000,000 less capital, and the person receiving it $50,000,000 more, than either had before. So with all money (except coin). It has no value in itself. It adds nothing to the capital of the world. It purports to be and is only a title to property, — a convenient device for transferring the ownership of property.

CHAPTER V.

BORROWER AND LENDER.

The man who loans capital to another, necessarily becomes the partner of the borrower in the business in which the borrower uses the capital borrowed. Whatever term is used to describe the compensation which the lender receives from the borrower for the use of his capital, whether it be premium, interest, rent, or profits, they all mean the same thing, namely, that the lender is to receive a part of its increase *as capital*, while it is in the hands of the borrower. This does not mean increase of the capital unaided by the endeavor of the borrower. Capital becomes such by being united to man's skill and intelligence. There is no form of capital that can exist for a moment, as capital, after man's vivifying power is withdrawn. It thereby loses its character as capital and becomes as the rocks and as the sands of the desert.

What would New York be, if to-night every human being should leave it and all its wealth, never to return? Its vast wealth would be as nothing. Though it should never decay, it would, as capital, be as though its surrounding waters had swallowed it up forever.

The necessities, the comforts, the luxuries, the innumerable advantages of every kind secured to the wage-worker of to-day, in the form of the compensation he receives from his employer, come very largely from the advantages furnished to this generation by the wealth accumulated by the generations that have preceded it. The difference between the condition of the barbarian and the average wage-worker of to-day (who is temperate, industrious, and frugal) is the measure of what the wage-worker daily receives from capital accumulated before his day. Only a modicum of the actual benefits of capital are exclusively enjoyed by its owners, or are paid by the borrower to the lender for its use. The great bulk of its earnings are commonly enjoyed by all.

In speaking of the *natural* increase of capital we include the power that vitalizes it. The terms commonly used to describe the compensation which the lender receives tend to confuse the mind. The one word which conveys the most correct idea is *rent*.

A man always borrows something of intrinsic value. What he borrows is not a piece of paper, whatever may be on it, but a farm, a house, a factory, or a part of them; a store, a mine, or goods. No man can borrow or lend anything else. The borrower gets from the lender what puts him in possession of the thing he seeks, and it must be some one of these things. Whatever becomes of the piece of paper which he took from the hands of the lender, or however soon it disappears, the borrower has the real thing borrowed, until he returns it or its equivalent to the lender. The inducement to the lender to part with his capital for a time is the belief that the borrower can do better with it for him than he can do for himself. The inducement to the borrower is the belief that the increase on the capital borrowed will be more than the rent for it which is demanded by the lender.

Any attempt by legislation to interfere with the buying, selling, or renting of farms, houses, factories, stores, or mines, is now never suggested excepting to secure justice to the weak. It has been proved by a thousand trials, that any interference by legislation with the price at which any goods shall be sold, invariably increases their cost to the consumer, and it is now so plain that no one proposes it. But it is equally true of all property. Any one who borrows the capital to pay for half of his farm is joint owner and partner with the lender — the lender getting that share of the profits of the farm agreed upon as the rental for his half, until the borrower buys out his half at the price agreed upon; or failing to keep his agreement jeopardizes his ownership in the balance, precisely as do the partners in any other business. So with the joint ownership in a house. One man holds the titles and assumes all the chances of both loss and gain on the whole house, paying for only half; another pays for the other half with a conditional ownership with a fixed rental for his half of the house (his capital loaned), on which he has no chance of gain over the rental, and is guaranteed against loss.

Selling goods by the merchant, the price for which is to be paid on a future day, or loaning capital by a bank or by an individual to a trader or manufacturer, is taking a part ownership in his stock. The rental on the part owned by the merchant is called *profit*. The rental for the part owned by the banker or money lender is called *interest*, but the terms, profit, interest, and rent, mean the same thing.

CHAPTER VI.

INTEREST.

There is no more beneficent law of finance than that requiring the payment of rent for the use of capital. Abolishing interest would be the death of enterprise. By the rental paid for the use of capital, capital is put into the hands of every man who is believed by those who have accumulated it to have the skill to keep it safely and use it wisely. Every man who loans his capital to another is influenced in the rent he demands for it by three considerations : First, its security; second, the length of time on which the loan is made; third, the amount loaned ; the lowest rental for capital being received on loans the most perfectly secured, for the longest time, and the largest amount, these considerations governing in the order named. The highest rental is paid where the greatest risk is taken, the time is shortest, and the amount the smallest.

The high rate of interest paid for one day's loan of capital in the New York Stock Exchange, the high rate in the shop of the pawn-broker, and the low rate on government bonds, illustrate and enforce this rule. These inflexible laws of finance are in the interest of the mass of the people. It is in their interest, as it is in the interest of every man in the community, to have doubtful and hazardous enterprises kept within reasonable limit, by high rates of interest on capital ventured in them. Those industries which supply the necessities of, and furnish employment to, the mass of the people, secure what capital they need at the very lowest practicable rate. Being the longest established, on the most secure foundation, and needing the largest amount of capital, they secure it at the lowest rates, and are thereby enabled to pay higher wages and to sell their products at lower rates; while the newest and most uncertain enterprises pay the highest rental for capital, whether it be for the building of a house in an undesirable locality, or the erection of a mill to manufacture goods of doubtful value. No portion of the people are proportionately so much interested in the stability of all kinds of business as the wage-worker. To him it is a matter of daily bread.

The prohibition in this country of all entail of property, and the freedom of every man to dispose of his capital to any person in any manner and for any price they can mutually agree upon absolutely or conditionally, whether called loans or sales, induces hundreds to loan their capital rather than use it themselves. This freedom of capital is at the foundation of business prosperity. Like the governor on the engine, which is left free to expand and contract the circle of its movement, thereby keeping the working power of the ponderous machinery at its most effective point, so the compensation paid for the use of capital is the governor of the stupendous movements of finance. Its freedom to increase and to decrease, as the enterprises constantly pressing for its use are safe or unsafe, is the regulating power that keeps our financial system at its equilibrium. The reason of our prosperity, notwithstanding the laws of so many states attempt to interfere with the freedom of the movement of capital, is that these laws do not commend themselves to the conscience, and are against the interests, of the people, and are therefore inoperative. Their only effect, if perfectly obeyed, would be to make the cost of the capital employed in all enterprises, — the safe and the unsafe, the useful and the useless, — the same, raising the rate of interest to those great and fundamental enterprises which now secure their capital at the lowest rate, thereby increasing the cost of their products to the consumer, and lowering it to the doubtful or chimerical enterprises which use up and practically destroy capital, for a time, in enterprises soon dead.

It is not for the interest of the public that enterprises which for to-day prove visionary and unprofitable, should be absolutely stopped, because they almost invariably prove ultimately useful in developing the resources of the country. The only practical way that finance has found to keep them in proper proportion to the immediately useful and necessary, in an experience covering centuries, is by the restraints of higher rates for the use of capital thus employed.

Very few writers on finance now dispute the proposition that any restrictive interference with the mobility of capital results in injury to the mass of the people. To-day, as compared with a century ago, capital seems almost liquefied. Investments were never before so insecure to the individual, and never so permanent to society. Capital was never so equally distributed, was never increasing so rapidly, and the mass of the people was never so secure in its use, enjoyment, and possession as now.

In bringing this to pass, and in all the progress we have made in commercial exchanges, banks have been a safe and indispensable agent, and none of them more so than those established under the present National Bank Act.

CHAPTER VII.

BANKS A NECESSITY.

THE business of the banker is as simple and as easily understood as that of the merchant, the manufacturer, the trader, or the farmer; it is just as legitimate, just as necessary, just as indispensable. The farmers all over the world produce the raw material, the merchants collect this raw material (buy it), and also distribute manufactured articles to traders (sell to them). The manufacturer takes the raw material from the merchant (buys it of him) and converts it into the forms in which it is consumed. The trader distributes it (sells it) to the consumers, — wage-workers and farmers, — taking from the farmer in exchange the raw material, which he sends to the merchant, and from the wage-worker the obligations against the banks, (bank-notes), which the manufacturer or farmer gave him for his labor.

These exchanges of property cannot be made, unless they are accompanied by some means of exchanging the titles to the property exchanged. This is easily accomplished without bankers, where the property of A. is desired by the neighboring farmer B., and B. desires the property of A. But when the farmer in Calcutta wishes to exchange his raw material for the goods manufactured in Birmingham, he must go through the whole circle of trade and manufacture, and the assistance of the banker is required by each one of the thousands who compose this circle in order properly to exchange and adjust the titles of each one of the thousands to his share of the property, at each stage of its progress. So, too, when the farmer in Iowa wishes to exchange his raw materials for the cloths of Lowell.

Each exchange of property (not primitive barter) is accompanied by two papers: one is given by the seller to the buyer, which is a certificate that the property described in it has passed from the possession of the seller to that of the buyer, and is called a bill of sale, which vests the title to the property in the buyer. The other is given by the buyer to the seller, and is a title to an equal amount of the property of the buyer, or some other party, and is called note, draft, check, bank-note, etc., as the case may be. This exchange of titles completes the transaction between these two parties. At this point in the transaction the assistance of banks is indispensable, for without the assistance of the banker it would be impossible for the seller to come in possession of the property to which he has accepted a title in exchange for the property he has just parted with.

CHAPTER VIII.

GOVERNMENT BONDS.

THE fact that banks are required to deposit with the United States treasurer government bonds, to secure against loss the holders of the promissory demand notes issued by the banks, may mislead some honest people as to the true character of these bonds; it may, therefore, be well to state exactly what the bonds issued by the United States government really are, before proceeding to examine the workings of the national banking system.

The United States bonds were given for and now represent property actually received from individuals by the United States government. Certain individuals voluntarily surrendered the whole or a large part of their property to the whole people (namely, the government), in the day of their necessity, but for which voluntary surrender of their property by individuals the government would have been compelled, at that time, to take by force from all the people the same amount of property as that voluntarily surrendered by the few, taking from each person that fraction of his property which his whole property bore to the property of all the people combined (taxes). The amount then needed was so large as to make it impracticable to immediately collect it by taxation.

Some individuals could surrender all their property without seriously disturbing society or themselves; but all could not give up so large a part without bringing disaster on all. Each person at the time he voluntarily surrendered his property received for it from the whole people (the government) their solemn obligation (United States bonds) to contribute from their property from year to year (taxes) an amount sufficient to return to him, on a certain day in the future, a specified amount of property as the equivalent of that voluntarily surrendered by him to the government; until which day the government further agreed to pay to him, quarterly, a sum agreed upon for the use of the capital surrendered.

These government bonds are, in essence, titles to a fraction of the property of each and every person in the country, who thankfully gave the title to this fraction of his property at the time the bonds were made, that he might thereby save the balance; each individual is personally indebted to the holders of these bonds because of the voluntary surrender of his property which the bondholder then made in place of *his* surrender. Each of them has had and enjoyed the fraction then saved to him, and its increase from that day to this.

The United States bonds are an admirable security for the circulating demand notes of national banks, or for any other obligation; but they are

GOVERNMENT BONDS.

not money. They fulfil none of the conditions of money. They represent uncollected taxes, — a lien on property. They represent fixed and not quick capital. They have no rightful place in banks of discount, except as security for business notes, and, to a limited amount, as a special reserve. The whole theory and practice of banking is the dealing in titles to property *in transit* that quickly mature. Government bonds are the exact opposite.

CHAPTER IX.

NATIONAL BANKS.

A BANK is made by five or more persons, who, desiring to begin the business of banking, put into a common fund the whole or a certain part of the capital of each, sufficient to make up the required amount, say $100,000, each taking from the custodian of the fund a paper which states what proportion of the whole capital of the bank belongs to him.

Having the requisite capital, the next step is to purchase so much of the obligations of the United States (government bonds) as the law requires the bank to deposit to secure the circulating promissory demand notes it applies for. Surrendering these bonds to the secretary of the United States Treasury, not absolutely, but in trust for the benefit of the whole people and the bank, the bank gets from the United States treasurer notes *in blank*, ready for its officers to sign, to the amount of ninety per cent. of the bonds surrendered, so made and printed that they cannot be counterfeited.

These blank notes are of no more value than waste paper when they are received from the treasurer of the United States by the bank. They are to the bank exactly what any blank note is to the merchant. But when they are signed by the proper officers of the bank they then have the full value stated in them; that is to say, they are worth just as much as and no more than any other promissory demand note, the payment of which is as thoroughly secured.

Calling them bank-bills, currency, or money, does not change the fact. All these terms are simply descriptive of the use to which they are put. The fact that they are promissory demand notes, and that only, is very carefully stated in the National Bank Act in the following words, namely: " Upon the transfer and delivery of bonds to the United States treasurer, etc., the association (bank) shall be entitled to receive circulating notes, *in blank*, to the amount of ninety per cent. of the bonds so deposited. After any such association (bank) shall have caused its (blank) promises to pay . . . to be signed . . . in such manner as to *make them obligatory promissory notes, payable on demand*, such association (bank) is authorized to issue and circulate the same as money."

Thus it appears that it is stated, as clearly as it is possible to state it, that the government assumes no responsibility for the issuing of national bank notes. It prohibits the bank from issuing its notes for more than ninety per cent. of the aggregate amount of United States bonds deposited by it with the United States treasurer to secure its circulating notes; and in order to be absolutely certain that this restrictive provision of the National Bank Act is complied with, it prints the blanks for the national bank notes itself. Here its responsibility begins and ends.

It is true that the government has its bonds, but it holds them as the trustee of each individual who has in his possession any national bank notes, and not for the banks. The title of the bank to them is secondary. It is a restrictive measure upon, and not in the interest of the bank, but in the interest of the people who take the notes of the bank. It is true the government is paying interest on its bonds to the banks that deposit them as security for their circulating notes, and the banks are paying no interest on their circulating notes. The banks do, however, pay back to the government what is equivalent to full interest on the untaxable bonds that secure their circulating notes. By an ingeniously contrived system of taxing the business of the banks, so as to collect taxes from each of them, not in proportion to the amount of the circulating notes each has issued, but in proportion to the amount of business done by each, the national and state governments receive from the banks, as a whole, more money than four per cent. interest on the aggregate national bank notes outstanding.

The national bank notes outstanding October 27, 1880, amounted to $317,350,000. Interest on this amount at four per cent. would be $12,694,000; while the state and national taxes paid by the banks in 1880 amounted to $14,619,000. This statement shows the profit to the government of its connection with the banks. The equivalent of taxes on the bonds is also collected at each time the interest on the bonds is paid, by the rate of interest the government pays on them, being less by just the amount of the taxes, were the bonds taxable. The government bonds specify that they are not again taxable; but the government receives a considerable sum, in taxation, more than the interest on the bonds deposited by the banks through the operations of the national banks under the National Bank Act.

Whether this is for the best interests of the people, is not so clear. Banks were not invented or created by the government. They existed long before the United States government was created, and may exist long after it has passed away. It is entirely proper, and the duty of the government, to take from the banks in taxes a sum equal to the pecuniary benefit conferred upon them by the government, and to provide all the safeguards necessary to prevent the banks from cheating the people by means of the " promissory notes " (money) they issue, or in any other manner; but any interference further than that must result in mischief.

The National Bank Act gives a very complete description of the work done by a bank. It says having been qualified to do so, a bank may "carry on the business of *banking*, namely, by discounting and negotiating promissory notes, drafts, bills of exchange, and other evidences of debt; by receiving deposits; by buying and selling exchange, coin, and bullion; by loaning money (its property) on personal security; by obtaining, issuing, and circulating notes, according to the provisions of this act." Every one of the things specified, as proper for a bank to deal in, excepting coin and bullion, is a title to property "in transit." In fact, national banks can deal in nothing else with safety. They have dealt in government bonds, it is true, but under special protection and exceptional conditions. So large a portion of the capital used in their business is upon "call" (deposits) that the titles they take for their loans must be of fixed value and to property that they can quickly realize on. The average unexpired time before they will come in possession of the property, the titles to which they receive in exchange for their capital (their loans), does not much exceed thirty days.

The word *bank* means bank of discount, not a trust company, whether called Savings Bank, Life Assurance Association, Loan Association, or by any other name. All of these only deal in titles to real or fixed property. They belong to a different guild, and are not like and have no more connection with institutions engaged in banking than do individuals who loan capital on real estate and like property. The National Bank Act prohibits "banks" from dealing in titles to, or loaning money upon real estate. It confines the banks to dealing in titles to property "in transit." They cannot lawfully invest one dollar in any property whatever not "in transit."

Property in transit is any property between the producer and final consumer. A cooking stove is "in transit" until it comes into the possession of the family. A machinist's lathe is "in transit" until it becomes the property of the man who is to use it to make other machinery. Every form of personal property is "in transit" until it reaches the hands of the man who buys it to use, not to sell again.

Experience proves that without legal prohibition banks will allow their capital to accumulate in fixed property to the injury of the great manufacturing and distributing interests, deranging the exchanges of the country and throwing workmen out of employment; and for this reason they are restricted to dealing in titles to property in transit.

The requirement of reserves in greenbacks, bank balances, circulation, etc., by the bank act, is very necessary for the security of the bank. It is necessary that bank officers know their proper proportion and substance, but they need not be discussed here. Their effect upon the business of banking, as of all restrictions, is to increase or diminish safety in the conduct of its business, and to increase or diminish the cost to the community of the services which it is obliged to have from banks.

CHAPTER X.

BANKS IN THE INTEREST OF THE PEOPLE.

THE government (the people) derives almost incalculable advantages from requiring that the banking capital of the country, to secure the circulating demand notes of the banks, shall first be invested in government bonds. It gives security to the government debt. The integrity of the government is by this arrangement so interlaced with every interest in the country, that the dullest intellect cannot fail to see that the repudiation of the government bonds would strike every man having a national bank note, making it clear to his pocket if it does not to his head, that the violation of the public faith, as well as private, is not only a disgrace to Christian civilization, but an immediate loss to every citizen.

Again, it gives to all the national bank notes a uniform and certain value all over the country, thereby lessening the excessive rates of exchange between one part of the country and another, which are unavoidable under any system of banking controlled by the states. Under the old state banking system the price of exchange sometimes reached above ten per cent. between Chicago and Boston.

This unnecessary tax upon the industries of the country cost the country millions of dollars annually, every dollar of which came directly from the pockets of the people, in the increased price which every trader was obliged to ask for his goods, in order to reimburse himself for this loss. It also secures a much lower rate of interest for the use of capital, by the feeling of security which it inspires, as it ministers very greatly to the stability of all the operations of business and social life, thus cheapening the cost to the consumer of every article he buys.

Still again the difference in value of sales to and purchases from one section of the country by another, in certain seasons of the year, and in certain products, is counted by millions, but the beneficent working of the banking system saves the shock and strain of these immense variations in a given season of the year, locality or department of commerce, by so adjusting the supply of capital to the demands of time and place as to lessen materially the total amount of capital required. This also cheapens production, enabling the masses to secure the things they consume at a less price.

But for banking every man in business would be obliged to keep about him, throughout the whole season, all the capital he needed to use at that part of the season when he required the most capital. That is to say, he must at all times have on hand the maximum of capital necessary, and any excess of that needed for present wants would be profitless when he was not using it. All the earnings that could be got from any body of capital that without banking must remain idle, must be added to what the article for the production of which the capital was kept idle now costs the final consumers, the large majority of whom are wage-workers.

Take the cotton crop, for example. When the cotton crop is ready to be sent to market, the whole body of farmers who produce it probably owe a sum equal to the value of the whole crop. That is to say, the amount of money left in the hands of the cotton-growers as a capital with which to grow another crop is no more than they, as a body, owe on their realty. The value of the raw cotton in 1870 was about $125,000,000. With no banking, this sum must have been in the hands of the cotton growers all the year, or the crop must be reduced to that amount of capital they permanently had. So of wheat, $245,000,000. So of manufactured products. Without banking each man doing any kind of business must have, all the time, as much capital as he needs at the time when he requires the most capital.

Whoever furnishes to another anything of intrinsic value, cloths, tools, seeds, animals, etc., "on time," furnishes capital to the value of the thing sold on credit; and the seller must deplete his working capital by so much, or secure a like volume of capital from a third party (usually the banks), and so on. Each man in business must have, of his own, on the average, the amount of capital of his minimum needs. The balance he uses, in most

BANKS IN THE INTEREST OF THE PEOPLE. 47

cases, is ultimately furnished by the banks. Banking makes nearly every dollar of the capital in the country productively available every day in the year.

It generally obscures, rather than serves to make clear, a subject to burden its discussion with statistics; but this point cannot be made so clear by any process of reasoning, as by stating the work performed daily by the capital each man in business is obliged to have in advance of its immediate use by him, which is now aggregated in deposits in the banks, and which would inevitably be idle but for banking.

The capital of all the national banks, including their undivided earnings, is about $600,000,000. The people have placed in their hands capital they do not need, for one day or more (deposits), about $900,000,000 more. Total, $1,500,000,000. The banks have loaned to individuals $1,300,000,000. Taking all the banks in the country on any given day and the unexpired time on $1,000,000,000 of this loan will average about thirty days (the other $300,000,000 loan is reasonably permanent, being on their own circulating notes). This loan averages about sixty days each, and is renewed six times a year.

A few men have about the same amount of capital, borrowed from the bank, every day in the year. Others borrow for one department of their business at one time, advancing it to their customers in the form of credit on the goods they sell, and for another department, representing a different raw material, at another time. Taking it all in all the $900,000,000 of bank deposits undoubtedly do the work which it would require $6,000,000,000 of capital to do in addition to what the country now has, were banks to make no loans on deposits. As agents for facilitating the use of capital not immediately needed by its owners, they are the means of very materially cheapening the cost of all the products of the country.

The banking capital in Worcester, Mass., a city of 60,000 inhabitants, is $2,200,000. The bank deposits average about $2,500,000. The average time each dollar deposited remains on deposit is about ten days, and the exchanges annually made through these banks are about $100,000,000. In fifty-six New York banks with a capital and surplus of $90,000,000, the deposits average about $270,-000,000. The average time each dollar deposited remains in bank is about two days, and the value of the exchanges made by these deposits is about $50,000,000,000.

If each one dollar deposited in banks in the United States remains three secular days, the exchanges made by the $900,000,000 deposited would be $90,000,000,000. Whether the figures given are correct or not, it is certain that the capital which each business man in the country thinks prudence requires him to have, in advance of the necessities of the day, when aggregated, is an immense sum, and the work done with it by banking equals the addition to the capital of the country of many times that amount.

There is no pretence that all the property "in transit" that passes from one person to another during a year aggregates more than about one third the sum named as the exchanges of *titles to property* made by the banks. It must be remembered that there are immense transactions in all forms of titles to property, where the property itself is not moved. Although these bank deposits average to be all drawn out every three days, in equal proportion each day of the three, the deposits as surely average to be renewed in three days, and each is going on at the same time, thus giving this aggregate deposit the character of a permanent loan, as the human body is said to be renewed each seven years while keeping its integrity. Perhaps a better illustration is the passenger traffic. Trains are run at various hours, full each way, run with a reasonable certainty of being full, when that result depends upon the voluntary and selfish action of isolated persons.

Think for a moment of its effect upon its business interests if each man in the country attempted to draw out of the bank the balance due him (his bank deposits) and keep it out twenty-four hours, a total of about $1,000,000,000. It would produce a commercial disaster that no man can conceive of, much less estimate; and yet we proceed with as much assurance of safety in this department of human affairs as in any other, in fact with greater safety.

Taking it all in all, the world over, there is no other department in which we can so safely calculate the future; where we have so strong an assurance that what has been will be. On the great sea of finance the wrecks of the fortunes of individuals who bid defiance to its laws are found on every hand; but the transactions of the world — from the check sent by the smallest country trader to the city merchant, to the floating of millions of the national debt; from the pay for a load of wheat the country farmer takes to the country store or railway station, to the pay for the cargoes of the navies of the world — ride on her bosom in a security as nearly perfect as is found in any human affairs.

The financial system is of the most delicate organization, so delicate that the slightest breath disturbs it; yet it is tougher, more stable, more enduring than all other human institutions. The fears of its servants do not arise from the workings of the natural and beneficent laws of finance, but from the meddling of alien or ignorant hands.

No financial contrivance of the present time is any more thoroughly the natural product of past experience than the national banking system of the United States. Every consideration urges its extension, with some slight modifications, to the extent of supplying *all* the circulating demand notes, as it does now all the banking facilities required by the business of the country. Its creation was but the putting into the form of statute law the recognized conditions of safe banking, and prohibiting any other. The universal acquiescence and approval of the system recognizes the certainty of the continuance of what now is, because it is the result of inexorable business.— laws of ages of business habits.

There is no department of business in which its habits, rules, and obligations are varied so little from year to year, and even from century to century, as in that of banking. The operations of none are more simple, and none require more nerve, penetration, promptness, and integrity. It beneficently binds every one of its members and all business men to implicit obedience to their promises. The unwritten banking laws of the ages justly prescribe the conditions upon which men may take part in making the exchanges of the country, while only helping their endeavor.

Any man can enter the circle of business, and remain there as long as he obeys its laws. He cannot stay there one day after violating them. If his obligation, for which he has pledged his honor and his property, is not satisfied on the day named, the announcement of his failure is flashed to the ends of the country. From that moment he can neither buy nor sell, and business men no longer recognize him as one of their number. If he returns to the guild of business he must enter as a new-comer.

CHAPTER XI.

INDUCEMENT TO ENGAGE IN BANKING.

THE inducement to engage in banking is the same as that in all other business, namely, the expectation of making more money by doing that business than by doing any other they care to engage in. Whatever capital is used to make a bank existed as real or personal property, or title to property, and before the bank was made, by bringing it together, afforded an income to the five or more individuals who made the bank.

It is purely a question of the use one will make of a specified amount of capital. By no legerdemain can one use the same capital for two purposes at the same time. The possession of *capital* gives one more or less *credit*. Credit does not mean the power of getting something, which having does not lessen what another has. Any *use* of credit is the borrowing by one man from another of his capital, the having of which by the borrower lessens the capital the lender has by just the amount loaned. Every man understands that any one who puts $50,000 into the mining business, or manufacturing business, or mercantile business, has that much less to use in any other investment.

INDUCEMENT TO ENGAGE IN BANKING.

It is precisely the same with banking. Capital invested in the banking business is *in banking*, and cannot be used for anything else until it is *got out* of the business of banking.

The profit on banking will average no more, covering a period of years, than that on any of the other kinds of business requiring the same skill and judgment. The banking business may be entered into with the same freedom as any kind of manufacturing, mining, farming, or any kind of trade. Every restriction put upon it by the law is one to protect the people from being cheated by the incompetency or dishonesty of those engaged in banking; not to hinder any one from doing the business of banking, or to help any one who undertakes it.

There is not a provision in the law intended to obstruct in the least honest and safe banking by any who desire to do it; or that gives the banking business any advantage whatever over any other business. Putting capital together to make a bank or trust company is in answer to a real or supposed demand for its use in that business, which is as promptly and freely complied with, and for the same reason that an additional factory is built, or an additional acre of ground is planted to wheat or corn; and banks are, to-day, just as necessary.

How many banks we shall have, where they shall be located, and how much capital they shall have, can only be rightly settled by the unrestricted operation of the law of supply and demand. No government, no association of bankers, no body whatever can be so circumstanced as rightly to settle this question. To attempt it is to do violence to the best interests of the community.

Free banking is our only safety. It is purely a question of what proportion of the whole capital of the country shall be devoted to the holding of the titles to property "in transit," and this, in the nature of the case, can only be determined by experiment. Inventions are so rapid, and the conditions of trade so variable, that this question, like all other purely business questions, must be left to the free action of the people without governmental interference. If there are too many banks, the capital invested in them will not make as good return to its owners as that invested directly in farming, manufacturing, or trading, and it will be withdrawn from banking and devoted to some other business. If capital invested in banking is more profitable to its owners than that invested in other pursuits, it will be taken out of those pursuits and put into banking.

Capital, like water, is always pressing with all its power to secure a common level for its whole volume. The competition between bankers is as sharp and persistent as between persons engaged in any other business; and their charges for the services they render are kept down by it as in all other business, as the reports of their profits, open to all, fully prove. That a bank is a necessity, will be made more clear by examining more carefully the work it does.

CHAPTER XII.

PRACTICAL WORKING OF A BANK.

(1.) A BANK buys (receives on deposit), besides coin and bullion, all the titles to property deliverable " on demand " (heretofore described as the merchant's cash), which come into the hands of every man in its neighborhood engaged in any kind of trade or business; in place of which it gives each depositor a title to a like amount of the property of the bank, to be satisfied on demand.

(2.) It takes from any person, anywhere in the world, any perfect title which he may have to any property, in the hands of any other person living anywhere in the world, and collects the equivalent of the property, and turns it over to the depositor.

(3.) It buys every "good" title offered for sale to property "in transit," where the title to the property is not perfect until a certain specified day in the near future (notes on time), if the capital in its possession is sufficient to do so. The bank usually requires, in addition to the title bought, that the seller give the bank a title to a like amount of his own property by writing his own name on the back of the note (indorsing it). Of course the title is purchased at a price mutually agreed upon.

The difference between its nominal value and the price paid for it by the bank is called "discount," and the buying of the note, draft, bill of exchange, etc., is called "discounting it." C. in Chicago sells a thousand bushels of wheat to B. iu Boston for $1,000. As soon as C. delivers the wheat and hands a bill of sale to B., C. has no more claim to the wheat than any other man whom B. owes. And B., by the act of accepting it, has delivered to C. a title to a thousand dollars' worth of his property. This title that B. gives is in the form of a check, draft, bill of exchange, etc. It calls for the immediate delivery of the thousand dollars' worth of property, or in the form of a note may call for its delivery at a fixed day in the future. It may call for its delivery in Chicago, or in Boston, or in London. The general rule is to make the check, draft, note, etc., payable at the place of business of the buyer.

Again, D. in Boston sells forty cases of boots to E. in Chicago for $1,000, which is done on the same day and upon the precise relative conditions that the wheat is sold. It is plain that these transactions balance each other. Whatever papers are passed, their practical significance is to demonstrate that fact. All trade the world over is identical with the balancing transactions described, however remote or near the buyer is to the seller, or the specified day of payment. Every man, every town, every city, every country, can buy only by selling an equal amount. If the sales of property "in

PRACTICAL WORKING OF A BANK. 57

transit" from Boston to Chicago exceed like sales from Chicago to Boston, the difference must be paid in coin or by the transfer of the ownership of titles to property not "in transit," from citizens of Chicago to citizens of Boston (supposing all titles held in each city to property "in transit" had been exhausted). This requires the going outside of the domain of banking proper, and of commerce proper, into that of the trust companies and real estate. This operation takes capital heretofore devoted to holding property "in transit" and puts it into fixed property. The changes of capital from real estate to property "in transit" and the reverse, are always being made, but in ordinary times they relatively balance each other. It is impossible to use any capital in real estate that it is necessary to use in handling property "in transit." The line of division between the two classes of property is as distinct if not as discernible as the dividing line between the United States and the British Empire, and the interchange between them is governed by the same laws.

The title to property taken by any and every bank, the world over, not satisfied at the counter of the bank first receiving it, is finally cancelled at the clearing house.

CHAPTER XIII.

CLEARING HOUSE.

There is no device of banking that is so perfect an epitome of, and so thoroughly illustrates, its workings (excepting the loaning of its property which differs in no respect from the loaning of capital by one individual to another), as the "clearing house"; which is used locally in most cities, and so far as the public is concerned, by its connection with all other clearing houses, unites all the banks of the city, the country, and the world into one bank.

Usually each bank in town or city connects itself with banks in one or more cities other than New York, and thereby becomes a part of the clearing-house system of those cities; and each is connected with some New York bank, and through that connection becomes a part of the New York clearing house. The New York banks, through private bankers, branches of foreign banking houses, connect themselves with London. So that each bank in the world is indissolubly connected with every other bank in the world, and in London is the final clearing house of the world.

The clearing house, in small cities, is usually

some one of the banks, with which every other bank deposits a small percentage of its capital. This deposit does not practically lessen the capital of the bank making it, for the reason that the deposit there made is counted as a part of the reserve of the bank making it that the law requires it to keep. At a certain hour of each day a boy from each bank meets at the "clearing house" a boy from each of the other banks, each having every check that the bank he represents has paid during the day upon any bank in the city other than itself. With his package of checks each boy presents a "clearing house" memorandum having the name of every bank printed on it, between debtor and creditor columns. Against the name of each bank, in the debtor column, the boy, before he leaves his own bank, enters the aggregate of all the checks his bank has in the package upon that bank, and carefully foots up the debtor column. The footing shows the total of the checks his bank has upon all other city banks, namely, upon the "clearing house." Each boy in succession calls off the total of the checks his bank has upon each of the other banks. As he calls them off, each of the other boys enters in the creditor column, against the bank calling, the total of the checks that bank has upon his bank. Having gone through the list, each boy adds up the creditor column. The difference between the creditor and debtor columns of the clearing house memorandum each boy has then shows the amount due the clearing house (all the other banks) from his bank, or to his bank from the clearing house.

Each of the boys then calls off to the clerk of the clearing house the totals of the debtor and creditor columns of his memorandum, which the clerk enters in his records. After each boy receives and verifies the checks each of the other banks has against his bank, each gives a check to, or receives a check from, the clearing house, as the balance may appear, and the work of the clearing house is finished for that time.

In Worcester eight boys, from seventeen to twenty years old, meet each day around a table in the directors' room of the clearing house bank and settle, in fifteen minutes, the business of its eight banks between each other for that day, amounting to about $125,000. The total coin and currency held by these banks average about $225,000, their daily transactions about $300,000.[1] In New York fifty-seven meet daily and settle in like manner the

---

[1] The clearing house in Worcester is made each day. It lives about twenty minutes and disappears. It has no capital. The bank acting for the clearing house receives from each bank from which a balance is due the clearing house its check on its Boston correspondent for the balance due the clearing house, and the clearing-house bank gives to each bank that has a balance due it from the clearing house its check on its Boston correspondent for that balance. Of course, the total of the checks given by the clearing-house bank and those received by it, balance each other less its own balance with the clearing house.

business the banks of that city have with each other, amounting daily to about $125,000,000. The total coin and currency held by the New York banks probably average about $75,000,000, and their daily exchanges are probably about $175,-000,000.

CHAPTER XIV.

BY WHOM MONEY IS MADE.

Money is necessarily made by individuals, not by the government. It is impossible for any government to make the money daily required by its people. To make the daily payments required by the trade of the United States, there are from $200,000,000 to $300,000,000 of paper obligations made each day by banks, and by individuals who have deposits in banks, which is money, as surely as any bank-note or greenback is money. It does the office of money for the day, and is destroyed at night. It is impossible to make the exchanges of the country unless the men who make them have and freely use the power of making the money they require. They cannot transfer the titles to and make payments for the goods they buy and sell without it.

Bank-notes or greenbacks, and much more coin, whatever their convenience for small and local transactions, are impracticable for the larger part of commercial transactions, for the reason that they are too cumbersome. It is impossible to have them at hand at all times and places they are needed. The inconvenience and cost of their transportation, small as is the percentage of that form of money now used, is a considerable inconvenience to and tax upon industry. Of the money daily used a very small percentage is bank-notes. The great bulk is checks, drafts, and telegrams. The telegraph transmits millions upon millions of bank credits from Boston to New York, Chicago, London, etc., etc., and the reverse, where the telegram is the only money used; no papers of any kind pass or are made, certainly none pass from one city to the other. The facts of the telegram are confirmed by letter. All that is done is to write, transmit, and deliver the telegram and make the proper entries on the books of the merchants and bankers interested. This money lacks no essential thing that the money issued by the banks has. If that described as made by individuals is not money, then that made by the banks is not money, for they are, in every respect, identical in substance. Trade in its present form is impossible without the continuance of the right which every man has now of making the money needed for his daily business, as far as he has the power to make it, which power is measured by his credit.

This is a part of the "inalienable rights of life, liberty, and the pursuit of happiness," reserved to the people in the United States Constitution, and the Constitution of every State, in substance if not in words. Congress has the same right and power to interfere with and "regulate" the use by the people of any of these forms of money that it has "to regulate commerce with foreign nations and among the several States," and no more. "To regulate" is the limit of its power. It has the same right to interfere to protect the weak and poor, from the strong and rich, in the department of finance, that it has in that of buying, selling, and transporting, because it is a part of it. The products of this country and of the world are as much "floated" by means of the various forms of transferring the titles to property used as money, as by the railway, the steamboat, and the canal, which transfer property itself. Congressional power over the forms of transferring titles to property (paper money) is found in the clause of the Constitution quoted above. By all rules of legal interpretation it is prohibited from issuing them to be used as money, by the limitations of the Constitution, in the words "to coin money, regulate the value thereof and of foreign coin." Congress is bound to exercise its power over the *titles to property* transported, within the letter of the Constitution, with the same cautious regard to private rights and interests that it observes in dealing with the question affecting the moving of property itself. All that Congress is asked to do by the people, all it has a right to do under the Constitution, is to stamp gold or silver, which is property, so that its weight and fineness may be known to all men, and to make such rules as will protect the people from being cheated by the forms of the titles to property, called money, which banks or individuals use.

Congress has no rightful power to "create" any form of paper money. The letter of the Constitution reserves to the people in their private or voluntary associate capacity this whole power of practical money, aside from the specified power granted to Congress, in the letter of the Constitution, to mould the precious metals into such forms as seemed to it desirable, and to stamp their weight and fineness upon them by any device it may choose to use.

CHAPTER XV.

IMPOTENCE OF STATUTE LAW.

GOLD is the soul of the financial system of the world. It is to money and banking what light and air are to life. In all the vast transactions of commerce it is the wand that ever reveals to all the exact obligations of one man to another, the world over. The power of municipal law to separate it from them, or in any respect materially to change or modify its relation to or power over them, is as impossible as would be an act of creation. To attempt it is to attempt to say by statute what shall be the thoughts and opinions of men, without changing any of the conditions that surround them, what shall be their motives of action, while acknowledging that all the things that go to make up inducements to act are beyond control.

How very small is the influence of that law which is enforced in courts of justice as compared with the habits and customs of daily life. The latter are more powerful than formal enactments, because they carry in themselves the means of their own enforcement. They are the very warp and woof of our existence. Such are the "laws of trade." They are as powerful as the mills of God,

IMPOTENCE OF STATUTE LAW.

and as prompt in their execution as the lightning's flash. Such is the power of gold over all commercial transactions. It is not by human enactment. It grows out of the absolute necessity of having some substance that in itself fully meets and satisfies the idea of value, implanted by God in the mind of man.

It is as impossible to conceive of, much less express, a definite value, without something in the mind that embodies and unerringly expresses it, as of a yard, without something in the mind of a definite length; or of quantity with no vessel or standard in mind that will measure quantity. It is as preposterous to deny the absolute power of gold to measure value, because value is a thing of the mind, or attempt to control it by statute law, as it would be to deny the existence of thought, because we cannot weigh thought in a balance, or to attempt to govern and regulate thought by act of Congress.

No law can be rightfully enacted which prescribes that any "money symbol" shall be a legal tender for all debts. Gold is not made a legal tender by the force of statute law. The law follows a usage. It does not make one. All commercial obligations agreed to deliver gold before statute law began, and it has continued in accordance with statute law and in spite of it down to the present time. It was made a legal tender by commercial usage, and no government has the power permanently to change it. The forming of gold into coin and declaring it a legal tender is the putting of the usage of the ages into a convenient and legal form, and nothing more. The purpose and power of coinage and legal tender acts are to prevent misunderstandings between the parties to contracts as to the exact weight and fineness of the gold, the delivery of which is promised in contracts and the saving of words in writing them.

The violation of the letter and spirit of the Constitution, by the enactment of a law to compel all creditors to accept government promissory demand notes in the place of the coin they were entitled to have in 1862, was not submitted to by the people because it was legally or morally right, but because of the resolve of every loyal man that no act of the government, honestly done, should be called in question in the face of a great national peril. But all contracts have been made from that day to this with reference to the amount of gold that the number of dollars mentioned in them would net. This is clearly shown by the fact that all articles that have a sale in Europe have sold here for the number of dollars that would net the same amount of gold here that the same things netted here when sold in Europe.

Providing by law that a man shall take any "money symbol" for his property, already sold or to be sold, is attempting to compel him to part with property which has intrinsic value for something which commands nothing of intrinsic value anywhere in the whole line of exchanges. This,

IMPOTENCE OF STATUTE LAW. 69

in the nature of the case, cannot be done because it is contrary to fundamental natural rights.

It is useless to waste words on hare-brained theories. We must assume that gold has in itself intrinsic value, that it is the most concentrated form of capital, and that it has the power to do what it has done since the world began, — measure the value of all other commodities by its own intrinsic value, as we are obliged to assume the fact of our own existence. Why or how it has this power has no more practical import in discussing financial questions, than how food nourishes the body has in the discussion of practical agriculture. It is certain that somewhere in the system of exchanging titles to property all values must be brought to a uniform and practical test, and this is only possible by making every commercial obligation, the world over, refer to and promise to deliver the same thing.

While every title exchanged, however small or however large, has reference to the delivery of a particular thing, or a promise to do a particular thing, there must be some provision made for the delivery of the thing, or the doing of the thing promised. Make it certain, or even probable, that the thing promised will not be delivered, or will not or cannot be done, and the whole edifice of finance will immediately come down with a crash. It is because of the perfect confidence of the business world that the gold will be forthcoming when called for, that the commercial edifice stands firm.

Gold is the foundation; integrity, ability, fidelity, industry, and promptness are the superstructure. It is all expressed in the one word "confidence," or in the sentence "confidence in our business associates." All the experience of the past and the facts of the present testify to the necessity of paying gold or its equivalent, in the settlement of every commercial obligation.

CHAPTER XVI.

CONCLUSION.

It appears then, (1.) that moneys are titles to property, the ownership of which or its equivalent passes with these moneys and is always in the person who for the time being holds them.

(2.) That coin, as distinguished from gold as property, and as used as currency, is the crudest and most inconvenient form of money, and is rarely used, only .81 of one per cent. of debts being paid in coin; and that nearly all of that small sum passes as property, rather than currency.

(3.) That greenbacks and bank bills are next to the lowest form of the money of commerce. That they are only used for the smallest and simplest transactions, only 4.6 per cent. of debts being paid in them.

(4.) That the great bulk of all payments, 95.13 per cent. of them, is made in checks, drafts, and other forms of money which are made by individuals, no piece of which continues in existence for scarcely more than a day.

(5.) That bank-notes can only be made to circulate to meet a specific and very limited demand; and can be made to do so small a part of the work of practical money, that the only needed restrictions upon their issue are the ones we now have; which simply secures, beyond a chance, their prompt payment by their maker on demand.

(6.) That no money is possible (excepting its circulation is compelled by might as against right) that has not in itself intrinsic value, or does not represent and is a title to property of intrinsic value. The aggregate of all paper moneys in circulation are titles to property of many times its nominal value. (The bank capital, United States bonds, signatures and indorsements on money, taking it all together, actually represent and make liable for its satisfaction more than ten dollars in value of *bonâ fide* property, for every dollar of paper money in circulation.)

(7.) That all capital used in banking is the aggregate of the capital of stockholders and depositors, and that banking is the exchanging of the titles to this property for titles to every kind of property that the community the bank serves desires to use, which are again exchangeable for others, and so on indefinitely.

(8.) That all forms of obligations used as money necessarily contain the option of having them converted into gold on demand, but that they are not *based* on gold exclusively, or to any large percentage. They are *based* on all the property, to which they are titles, which is in process of being exchanged. It is understood to be, and is, the opposite of credit. Money is passed to end a credit, not to make one. A. passes money to B., because he is indebted to B. The obligation of A. to B. may be one second old or one year. A. meeting B. says, " Will you lend me $1,000 for ten days?" "Certainly," says A. That instant B. has a credit with A. for $1,000. A. ends the credit by handing $1,000 to B. and receives for it a title to the property of B. maturing at the expiration of the ten days.

(9.) That the banking business is never done on credit as distinguished from capital. Credit, as that word is usually understood, forms no appreciable part of it. Money is *based* on the capital in process of being increased in volume and usefulness, in the factories and in the stores of the country — capital in transit. All the obligations of a bank are titles to actual capital, of which gold is a very small but absolutely necessary part.

What safety requires its proportion to the bank deposits to be, is determined by circumstances, and is constantly varying. That there must be a sufficient amount in any country to make it certain that the final balance between it and other countries,[1] and between its own banks, will be promptly paid in gold, in addition to the amount necessary to supply the wants of the financially timid or ignorant, is certain.

---

[1] The "final balance" is the balance due at any time, from one country to another, after they have for the time exchanged all those things which they then desire to exchange and can agree upon the terms of exchange.

The man who dares trust no man will hoard his accumulations in gold. The man who, migrating, does not know the use of safer and better ways, will carry his capital in gold, and so on. The more enlightened a people and the more complete its means of exchanging property and information, the less gold is required, proportionately and absolutely, which proportion is constantly growing less.

As there is no essential difference between bank promissory demand notes and any other form of demand against the property of a bank, there is no good reason for making any distinction between them and any other form of bank liability, in restricting their amounts by taxation or by any other disability.

The only effect of any such regulations must be to discriminate unjustly against that class in the community whose convenience compels them to use bank-notes. The liability of a bank is not increased one dollar by having them expressed by outstanding bank-bills rather than by its outstanding book accounts, checks, drafts, or liabilities of any other kind. Again, excepting at the season of the handling of the crop, the demand for bank-bills is very uniform, and any accumulation of them in any depository out of the reach of the people cannot fail to work hardship.

It is immaterial whether this hoarding is done for a good or a bad purpose, by an individual or by the treasurer of the United States; the effect upon the labor of the country is the same. It is clear that the interest of all is best served by the immediate deposit in banks of the capital any one has, not needed by him for immediate use, which bank-bills stand for and are titles to. All admit that if at any time all persons withheld, or attempted to withhold, such deposits, commercial ruin would immediately sweep over the country.

So far as its monetary transactions are concerned, the United States government is a huge business corporation. The same hardship is caused to the laboring men of the country by any disturbance of business caused by its action in violation of the inexorable laws of trade and finance, as would be caused by a private corporation or individual,— doing business of the same magnitude, — doing the same thing. That widespread ruin has not heretofore been caused by the operations of the United States sub-treasury, and by the issuing of legal tender notes by the government, proves the extravagant and wasteful methods of this country, to which the government is no exception, rather than the exemption of "the great American nation" from those maxims and laws that inexorably hold all other peoples.

Poisons may be taken and death not immediately follow, and even permanent injury may not always be done. Hundreds of men survive wounds that usually cause death. Reckless and unsound business methods, under exceptional circumstances, sometimes succeed for brief periods, where obedience to sound maxims and recognized laws fail; but a true and enduring prosperity is only secured to a nation or individual by a strict compliance with those laws which are approved by all human experience. They are such not by man's creation. They are a part of nature, discovered, not made, and can no more be continuously defied or ignored than the law of gravitation.

Scarcely any two things can be conceived of that are alike in appearance, that are more opposite in character or in their effect on the business of a country than the promissory demand notes of a bank (bank-bills) and government legal tender notes. Every bank-bill paid out by a bank is a title to the permanent property of the bank, in exchange for which the bank receives from the individual to whom it hands the bill, property, or a title to property, of a like amount. The property to which the titles have been thus exchanged is "in transit" quick capital, sure to be realized on at a time certain, and is set apart by the borrower to pay the loan of the bank.

A legal tender promissory demand note is a title to nothing. It has no permanent property set apart to pay it. It is always issued for property consumed or for property put into public buildings, river and harbor improvements, etc., etc., so that it cannot possibly be used to satisfy the obligation assumed when the legal tender representing it was issued. The legal tender has no duplicate title to quick property, or to anything else. It is a forced loan, to the injury of both parties to it. In its very

CONCLUSION. 77

best aspect, it is only a promise to exercise the sovereign power of taxation at some future time, the exercise of which must inevitably disturb all the business adjustments of the country to just the extent it is exercised.

In the return to the bank of the capital the individual borrowed of it (represented by the banknote he received from the bank), he surrenders to the bank the equivalent of that capital, either in titles to the property of the bank (bank-notes) or their equivalent. To the government, for its issue of promissory demand notes, nothing is promised or due.

In the case of the government, if it proposes to redeem promptly its promissory notes (legal tenders) it is obliged to keep sufficient capital to do so constantly on hand unemployed, to the great loss of the government (the people), — see the millions now idle in the United States treasury, — while the banks are loaning and deriving an income from their capital which their promissory notes (bank-bills) represent.

By the working of the known laws of banking they have a certainty that their capital will return to them, and be available (deposits) to meet their promissory notes (bank-bills) when they are presented for redemption. Again, the borrowing of the capital of the bank (bank-bills) is the securing the titles to *bonâ fide* capital of intrinsic value for a limited time, and at a sacrifice by the borrower of a portion of the profit secured by him by his use of this capital, in the form of a fixed rental for its use (interest). This rental operates as a limitation, to the actual necessities of the community, of the volume of bank-bills issued. It also operates as a constant pressure on the whole volume of bank-bills in circulation, to compel the return to and destruction by the banks of any surplus that may have been issued over the necessities of the people. This withdrawal of bank circulation does not depend on the will of the bank, but on the legitimate needs of borrowers.

Upon the legal tender promissory notes issued by the government every influence is the exact opposite of that on the promissory notes issued by the banks. There is no pressure upon the whole volume of government legal tender promissory notes to cause any portion of them to return to their source. Every consideration which seemed to justify their original issue inevitably operates, and with redoubled force, to prevent their return and to compel and justify a still further issue. Bank promissory notes are issued to meet the necessities of those receiving and using them and for a valuable and permanent consideration, representing property in transit, and are under the control of the certain and well-known laws of finance.

Government legal tender notes are issued to meet the necessities of the party making them, and for the exact opposite of a permanent consideration, and represent consumed property and in violation of all safe financial maxims. The existence of legal

CONCLUSION. 79

tender notes issued by any governments shows as reckless a disregard of well-understood financial law as a plague does of healthful sanitary conditions. Any redundance of legal tender notes must be absorbed by inflating prices, to the great injury of the wage-workers, for their volume is necessarily inflexible; while under our system there can be no redundance of national bank bills, exchangeable for gold on demand, because any surplus is retired by being paid into the bank in order to stop the rental on the capital they are titles to. This process is constantly going on. The struggle by one set of persons and influences to increase, and by another set to diminish, the volume of bank-bills in circulation, is as intense as self-interest can make it, the result being to make the supply exactly equal to the legitimate demand.

There is scarcely an existing government that has not tried the experiment of issuing legal tender notes, and there is not a single instance of its failing to inflate prices, bringing uncertainty of employment and positive suffering to the wage-workers, and only profiting, and that for a brief period, the reckless and unscrupulous speculators who are found in every department of business. On the other hand, there is no instance where the promissory demand notes (bank-bills) issued by banks, redeemable in coin, ever affected unfavorably any community that used them. Kept within their natural limit, injury from their issue is impossible, for there is a dollar's worth of property of intrinsic value especially pledged to meet instantly every one of them on demand. If the conditions of issue were the same as of government legal tender notes, the effect of their issue would be the same; but the conditions of their issue being the exact opposite, their effect is the exact opposite.

Let the government withdraw all the legal tender notes; they can work no good, and are a source of great danger; and the people themselves will supply all the circulating notes they can advantageously use, that are at all times interchangeable for gold. The issuing of currency by the government to the amount of any fraction of that permanently absorbed by the people, takes from the elasticity of the whole volume by just so much. In its least objectionable feature it is as effective and objectionable as it would be for a manufacturer to fill up his reservoir with stones, above its lowest outlet, to make the water run over the flash-boards, to supply his mill-pond below, when by simply raising the artificial obstruction, the gate, the water would flow of its own accord; or for him to put into his factory a steam-engine, to get more power where the heat and steam would be of no possible advantage to him, and where it was liable to do him very serious damage, when he could get the added power with perfect safety and at no expense by the action of the law of gravitation, by simply hoisting the water-gate of his mill-pond a little higher.

The only possible office of the government note is the doing abnormally and at great risk, a part of

CONCLUSION. 81

the work that the bank-note would naturally, safely, and better do. Besides its other vices, it has the vice of being an obstacle between the people and the gold they are entitled to "on demand." Now their demand for gold at the counter of a bank is answered by handing to them a greenback, and the gold for the paper handed them can only be legally demanded at a sub-treasury, perhaps a thousand miles away.

The one obstacle that stands in the way of a prompt withdrawal of all forms of government demand notes is the United States Sub-Treasury Act. Repeal that act and the path is clear to the entire withdrawal of the government from all interference with the finances of the country, excepting the exercise of its police power, the exercise of which, and only which, it has any warrant for in the Constitution.

Whatever may have been the condition of the banks of the country which seemed to justify the establishment of the sub-treasury, it is to-day the greatest curse that afflicts the finances of the country. It not only places duties, powers, and opportunities in the hands of the United States treasurer, such as no human being should ever be intrusted with, but it compels him to do what is made a misdemeanor, visited with severe penalties when done by a bank, and would not be submitted to for a day if done by an individual: namely, it locks up the money of the people. The making of any loan upon the security of United States or national bank notes, or agreeing for a consideration to withhold the same from use; in other words, the "locking up" of money, is made a misdemeanor, and the bank committing the offence is punishable by a fine of $1,000, and a further sum of one third of the money so loaned. The officers of the bank making the loan are also subject to a penalty equal to one quarter of the money loaned.

This provision of law is not applied to individuals, because locking up money is an offence they do not commit without the assistance of banks. These severe penalties were provided because the locking up of money was an injury to the public; and furthermore, the injury is in exact proportion to the amount of money locked up, and is not made any greater or less by the "locking up" being done by a bank, an individual, or by the United States treasurer.

Yet in the face of the enactment of a law by the United States government severely punishing a bank for withholding currency from circulation, it maintains the sub-treasury in violation of every sound maxim of finance, in violation of the laws governing the banks, and in the face of the damage to the industries of the country admitted to be done by it, every day of its existence, now necessarily inflating, and now necessarily curtailing the volume of the circulating medium, by the accumulation in, or the disbursements from, the treasury.

The absurdity, to call it nothing worse, of a government needlessly keeping the people in a chronic state of suspense and anxiety as to what the government treasurer will do, by compelling him by law to lock up from the use of the people the means necessary to the steady and safe conduct of the daily business of the country, or of putting the power to do so in the hands of any one of its citizens, with the certainty (in the light of the peculations heretofore practised by high government and private officials) that some one of them, by using his information and power, will sooner or later put millions in his pocket, cannot be matched by the financial action of any nation having a sound credit now in existence.

There is not a solid reason to justify the continuance of the sub-treasury for a day. Ample security can be furnished by the deposit of government or other solid bonds, by any one of a hundred banks, for every dollar the United States treasurer need deposit in them, and at any one of the points where it is desirable to keep the deposit. The people would then have the use of the capital accumulated by the United States government, in anticipation of its wants, in the form of "deposits in bank" to the credit of the United States government, as it now has the capital that every private citizen or corporation now has in advance of needs.

In the domain of finance the whole people acting as one, the United States government, is the peer of the humblest man who counts one in the great whole. It can avail itself of no power in the universe to raise itself above the level upon which each individual member of it stands. It can no more permanently control or modify the laws of finance, in its own behalf, than it can the law of gravitation.

The United States government, in all that pertains to finance, is a huge business establishment, and nothing more. The following table, compiled from the reports of the comptroller and United States treasurer, shows to what extent the operations of the United States treasurer, by locking up currency in the sub-treasury, needlessly disturbs the finances of the country. It further shows how needless is the further existence of the government legal tender notes, either to the government as a business corporation or to the volume of circulating notes. The vicious sub-treasury system, and government legal tender note system, complement and support each other, to the good of none and the injury of all.

That ample security in government or other bonds approved by the United States treasurer would be gladly furnished by banks situated at convenient points, for all the money the government would have to deposit, no one doubts. If this is true, there is no good reason for maintaining the sub-treasury. On the 30th day of September, 1879, if the United States treasurer had deposited in the banks all the funds in his hands and had called in and destroyed every legal tender note, the money in actual use by the people would have been reduced by only one million four hundred thousand dollars.

CONCLUSION.

DIFFERENT FORMS OF MONEY (IN MILLIONS) IN THE UNITED STATES TREASURY.

	Sept. 30 1876.	Sept. 30 1877.	Sept. 30 1878.	Sept. 30 1879.	Sept. 30 1880
IN UNITED STATES TREASURY.					
Gold	$55.4	$107.	$136.	$169.8	$135.6
Silver	6.	7.4	27.9	58.	78.7
Legal Tender	73.2	82.8	73.	48.8	27.9
Bank-notes	15.2	14.1	9.3	4.5	3.5
Total	$149.8	$211.3	$246.2	$276.1	$245.7
IN NATIONAL BANKS.					
Gold	$18.9	$19.	$24.7	$87.2	$102.8
Silver	2.5	3.7	5.3	5.	6.5
Legal Tender	84.2	66.9	64.4	69.2	56.6
Bank-notes	15.9	15.6	16.9	16.7	18.2
Total	$121.5	$105.2	$111.3	$128.1	$184.1
IN CIRCULATION.					
Gold	$74.8	$66.7	$86.7	$98.7	$127.
Silver	21.5	39.	47.1	63.4	67.1
Legal Tender	208.6	200.2	209.2	225.7	262.1
Bank-notes	290.1	287.	294.9	314.	322.1
Total	$595.	$592.9	$637.9	$704.8	$778.3
Legal Tender in Circulation	$208.6	$200.2	$209.2	$228.7	$262.1
Money in Treasury other than Legal Tender	76.6	128.5	173.2	227.3	217.8
Legal Tender in Circulation in excess of Money in Treasury.	$132.	$71.7	$36.	$1.4	$44.8

Whatever the necessities of the government were that were thought to justify the original issue of legal tender notes, it is now impossible for it to derive any advantage from continuing them, even if there were no objections to their use.

Taxation, as now exercised, draws from the banks more than the equivalent of the interest on every government bond pledged to secure the demand notes of the bank now in circulation.

It should be the aim of the government to so levy taxes as to increase the rate of interest as little as possible, as increasing the rate of interest most quickly checks production. Still there is no valid reason why the banks should not pay taxes to the equivalent of the especial advantages they derive from their connection with the government; or why capital, in the form of deposits in banks, should not be taxed so long as anything is taxed, other than property having intrinsic value; but the absurdity of laying any portion of the taxes on the promissory demand notes of the banks is unequalled. They are a part of the bills payable of the banks and that only. They are the checks, drafts, bills of exchange, etc., of the common people, and must not be taxed while the same thing used by another class are not taxed.

It is immaterial whether the obligations of a bank are in the form of outstanding " promissory demand notes " (money), or on deposit accounts, drafts, checks, etc., etc. The total indebtedness of a bank, and the certainty of its prompt payment on demand, is the only thing its officers or the public regard in adjusting the amount and character of its reserve.

The importing or exporting of gold, or the maintaining of specie payments by the banks, is affected less by their circulating demand notes than by any other form of bank obligation, because they are so much less in volume; and further, they are so necessary to the common transactions of every-day life that to collect and present them for payment in a sufficient amount to reduce permanently their volume, is impracticable.

Banks ought never to be short of currency. It is as unnecessary, under proper forms of taxation, as to be short of blank checks, drafts, etc. Have enough for the maximum needs, adjust the whole volume of taxation so as to produce the just amount of revenue from the banks, leaving bank-bills free from taxation, will accomplish that end.

To place the financial system of the country as far as practicable beyond the possibility of disturbance by the action of any one man, be he public officer or private citizen, and to make it as secure as possible, we need:

(1.) To abolish the whole sub-treasury system and require that all moneys received by the government shall be immediately deposited, at convenient points, in national banks. All banks at designated points should have the right to bid freely and publicly for the privilege of acting as depositories of public funds, and should furnish ample securities in government or other solid bonds for all deposits made in them by the government.

(2.) To redeem and cancel every dollar of government demand promissory notes.

(3.) To require the United States treasurer to act as custodian, free of expense to the banks, of all gold offered to him for safe-keeping by any bank, and to issue gold certificates therefor of any denomination desired in sums the multiple of five.

(4.) All reserves of banks to be in gold, gold certificates, or in bank balances, etc., as now. The banks to be prohibited from receiving on special deposit coin or bullion, and the prohibition of any loan on United States or national bank notes as security to be extended to coin and bullion.

(5.) Gold, or government gold certificates, to be legal tender for all debts, public and private.

(6.) The banks to pay taxes predicated upon their having each day a gold reserve to an amount equal to a certain percentage of their total deposits for the day.

(7.) As the gold in any bank rises above the prescribed amount, its taxes shall proportionately decrease, until the amount of gold the bank holds shall reach an amount equal to a specified percentage of their total deposits, above which percentage the bank shall reap no advantage in taxation by accumulating gold.[1]

---

[1] There is ample gold in the world for all its legitimate uses in commerce, provided it is free, within reasonable restrictions, to seek its trade level. Next to so arranging our financial system as to

CONCLUSION.

(8.) As the gold in any bank decreases below the required amount, its taxes shall proportionately increase.

(9.) When any bank fails to redeem on demand its promissory demand notes in gold, from that day its taxes should be increased to a penalty tax, which shall continue so long as the suspension of gold payments continues, or until a receiver is appointed.[1]

(10.) Each bank to select a bank at any one of several designated points, with the approval of the comptroller of the currency, at which it shall redeem its promissory demand notes, which redemption banks shall send to the New York redemption bank any bills received of banks outside of its circuit, to be thence sent to their proper circuit.

(11.) Mutilated bills to be sent to the United States treasury, for duplicates or for final redemption.

As all commercial transactions refer to and are measured by gold, it is necessary that a certain definite and unvarying part of them be actually made in gold, lest by long periods of non-use its power be underrated from its being obscured. The laws of mind are such that we cannot trust our-

---

fail to secure our fair share, is the arranging it so as to accumulate here an undue proportion. Hence the advantage to the banks of reduced taxation should stop when it has accumulated a reasonable amount.

[1] A bank should not be allowed to profit by failing to meet its obligations, and as the injury is done to the public, no exception can justly be taken by the bank to such a provision of law.

selves to estimate justly things long out of practical use and long out of mind. We cannot keep in health the financial tissues without the reasonable and constantly visible use of gold. It becomes more necessary to secure an arbitrary use that its place and power may be always recognized, as financial operations become more refined. Therefore the duties on imports should be invariably paid in gold or gold certificates.

Again, the accumulations of the whole body of the people should of right be in that form of property in which their obligations are discharged. If the gold is not collected and deposited in bank by the government, the people will soon fail to see the moral right of the government to demand gold of the banks to pay the interest on its bonds. But the master consideration for adhering to the policy of requiring all duties on imports, not only in form but in substance, to be actually paid either in gold or gold certificates, is because it is the only safety of the country in times of panics or long-continued commercial disaster. Without this most wise provision in our revenue laws it is impossible to have them operate justly in abnormal conditions.

Continuing our present policy of collecting all revenue on imports in gold, with the power in the hands of the United States treasurer to sell the bonds he holds as security for deposit, when gold is refused by the bank in answer to his demand, and his position is as secure with no sub-treasury as now.

CONCLUSION.

The only remaining question that my limits will permit any observations upon, is that of the recurrence of financial panics, — disturbances of the financial system so great as to cause the suspension of specie payment by the banks, etc. Will the adoption of the suggestions herein made be a remedy in the future for all panics such as have been experienced in the past? Yes! without the shadow of a doubt, — when hurricanes cease; when earthquakes are unknown; when railway and steamboat accidents are things of the past; when accidents never come to the prudent; when the unexpected never happens; when the operations of the known laws of the universe cease to be disturbed and apparently frustrated by the operations of the unknown.

All human conduct is based on the doctrine of chances. Do all that prudence dictates in the light of past experience, and rest it there, is the law in all the concerns of life. Progress is only consistent with holding in our conduct a just equilibrium between risk and security. But this fact does not justify or excuse any departure from well-settled principles or practices by an individual or government.

APPENDIX.

SUMMARY OF THE PRINCIPAL RESTRICTIONS AND REQUIREMENTS OF THE NATIONAL BANK ACT.

(1.) THE corporate powers possessed by the national banking associations, and which they cannot exceed, are limited by the organic act which governs them, and are very carefully enumerated therein. They are briefly as follows : —

First. To adopt and use a corporate seal.

Second. To have succession for twenty years, unless sooner voluntarily dissolved, or their franchise becomes forfeited by some violation of law.

Third. To make contracts.

Fourth. To sue and be sued, as fully as natural persons.

Fifth. To elect or appoint directors, and by the directors to appoint a president, cashier, and other officers, and define their duties.

Sixth. To adopt all necessary by-laws, not inconsistent with law.

Seventh. To exercise by their boards of directors, or officers, *subject to law*, such incidental powers as are necessary to carry on the business of banking ; by discounting and negotiating promissory notes and other evidences of debt ; by receiving deposits; by buying and selling exchange, coin, and bullion; by loaning money on personal security; and by obtaining and issuing circulating notes.

These are the entire powers possessed by the national banks, and it has been judicially held that all powers not here enumerated are withheld. These enumerated powers, therefore, operate also as restrictions upon the banks.

(2.) One of the provisions appearing in the above grant of powers is that the national banks may loan money upon personal security only — that is, real estate may not be taken by them directly or indirectly, as *original* security for any loan; the effect of which is to make them commercial institutions, and to discourage the loaning of money upon securities not readily convertible.

(3.) Mortgages on real estate may be taken, or real estate be conveyed to them, by way of security for, or in satisfaction of, debts previously contracted in good faith; or they may purchase the same at sales under judgments, decrees, or mortgages held by them. But all possession by them of such real estate, whether under mortgage, by purchase, or otherwise, is limited to five years.

(4.) They are required to have a paid-up capital of not less than $100,000 each, and in cities of 50,000 inhabitants their capital must be not less than $200,000 each. In the discretion of the secretary of the treasury, however, banks with not less than $50,000 capital may be organized in places having less than 6,000 inhabitants. The design and effect of these provisions is to prevent, as far as possible, the establishment of feeble organizations, unequal to the wants of the communities in which they are located.

(5.) At least one half of the authorized capital must be paid in before commencing business, and the remaining portion must be paid in at the rate of not less than one fifth monthly from the time the association is authorized to commence business. Proper provision is made for enforcing payment of installments of capital stock subscribed, or for making good any impairment of capital which may occur in the course of business.

(6.) The comptroller is also authorized and required, before issuing his certificate of authority to any association to commence business, to ascertain if such association has in good faith complied with all the requirements of law preliminary to its organization, and he may appoint a special commission for this purpose if thought necessary. He must also obtain a sworn statement of the president and cashier and of a majority of the directors of the proposed association, setting forth all the facts properly bearing on this inquiry.

(7.) No increase or reduction of the authorized capital of an association can be made without the approval of the comptroller being first obtained, and no increase is valid until the whole amount is actually paid in and certified to under oath.

(8.) Every director must be a citizen of the United States, and three fourths of the directors of any association must be residents of the state, territory, or district in which it is located. Each director must also, during his whole continuance in office, be the *bonâ fide* owner of not less than ten shares of the capital stock of the association of which he is a director, which shares must not be hypothecated or in any way pledged as security for any loan or debt. To all of which he must make oath.

(9.) Every director must also, immediately upon his election or appointment, make and transmit to the comptroller an oath that he will faithfully administer the affairs of his association, and will not knowingly violate, or permit to be violated, any of the provisions of the National Bank Act.

(10.) The shareholders of every national bank are each made individually responsible, equally and ratably, and not one for another, for all contracts, debts, and engagements of such association, to the extent of their stock therein, at its par value, *in addition* to the amount invested in such shares; thus giving a double security to the general creditors of these associations.

(11.) Each national bank, before it is authorized to commence business, must have first deposited with the treasurer of the United States an amount of interest-bearing, registered United States bonds, not less in any case than $30,000, nor less than one third of the paid-in capital of the bank, except that, by a late act, the maximum deposit of bonds required for any bank is $50,000. These bonds are primarily held as security for the redemption of the circulating notes of the bank; but as the amount of circulation issued equals ninety per cent. only of the par value of the bonds deposited, any excess in the value of the bonds above the amount of circulation to be redeemed becomes an added security, in the possession of the government, applicable to the payment of claims of the general creditors of the association depositing them, should it become insolvent.

(12.) National banks are forbidden to make transfers or assignments of any of their assets or credits after an act of insolvency, or in contemplation thereof, with a view to the preference of one creditor to another; and any transfer or assignment so made is null and void.

(13.) Every association in the national system is required to receive at par, for any debt or liability to it, the circulating notes of any and all other banks in the system, and these notes are also receivable by the government for all taxes or other dues, except duties on imports, and are payable for all debts or demands owing by the government, except interest on the public debt. These features give to the notes an additional value beyond that which they possess through a deposit of United States bonds.

(14.) One of the most invaluable features of the national banking system is that requiring each association to have at all times on hand an available cash reserve of specified proportions as compared with its deposits and circulation. The proportion required for banks located in the financial centres of the country is twenty-five per cent. of their deposits. For all other banks the required proportion is fifteen per cent. of their deposits. The proportion of reserve to circulation is the same for all banks, namely, five per cent., which amount is to be at all times on deposit with the treasurer of the United States, to be held and used by him in the redemption of their notes. This sum is also permitted to be counted as part of the required reserve on deposits. Most stringent means are placed at the disposal of the comptroller for enforcing compliance by the banks with the requirements of the law relating to the maintenance of a cash reserve.

(15.) Equal in importance with the requirements as to a

cash reserve are the provisions which compel the accumulation by each national bank of a surplus fund, to be set apart by it from time to time out of the profits of its business, and which fund may not be used by the bank for any purpose other than to meet and charge off losses in excess of its current earnings. These provisions require that each association shall, before making any dividend, carry to its surplus fund one tenth part of its net profits since its last preceding dividend, until the same shall amount to twenty per cent. of its capital stock. It is further provided, that no dividend shall ever be declared by any association to an amount greater than its undivided profits (not surplus) then on hand, deducting therefrom its losses and bad debts, and that if such losses shall equal or exceed its profits on hand other than surplus, no dividend shall be made. Careful provision is thus made for the steady growth of the surplus fund of each national bank, until its sum shall equal one fifth of the capital of the association, thereby establishing a reserve fund against which it may charge any excess of losses over and above its other profits on hand, and thus preserve its capital stock unimpaired. Under these provisions the amount of surplus accumulated by all the banks now in operation is $116,897,800, against an aggregate capital of $466,147,436.

(16.) Another very important feature of the law is the requirement that detailed statements of the condition of each national bank, verified by the oath of its president or cashier, and attested by not less than three of its directors, shall, not less than five times in each year, be made to the comptroller, and also be published in the city or town where the bank is established; and to guard against the possibility of any bank fortifying itself, in advance of a known day for making a report, so as to make a good showing on that particular day, it is further provided that each report shall be for some *past* day, to be specified by the comptroller. This office, also, under the law, makes annually a report to Congress, containing a great number and variety of statistical tables compiled from the various reports of the banks, through the wide distribution of which full information concerning the banks and the working of the system is annually placed before the public.

(17.) The national banks are also required to make semi-annual reports to the comptroller of their dividends declared, and the amount of their profits in excess of such dividends, which returns are also tabulated by him, and the results presented to Congress and the country in his annual reports. Full means are provided for enforcing compliance by the banks with the provisions of law concerning both classes of reports here named, by authorizing a severe penalty for any failure or neglect to make and transmit the same.

(18.) In addition to the means for acquiring a knowledge of the condition of the banks furnished by the reports already mentioned, the law provides for their examination periodically by disinterested persons to be appointed by the comptroller. These persons visit the banks, inspect their books of account, securities, and assets and liabilities generally, have power to examine their officers and directors under oath, and inquire into all matters necessary to a full understanding of their actual, existing condition, and then make immediate and full report in writing of the results of such examination. This feature of the law is an invaluable one, operating not only as a restraint against irregular practises by any banks so disposed, but as a means of detecting them and preventing their recurrence. These examinations may be as frequent as is thought necessary, and their expense is borne by the banks themselves.

(19.) All necessary publicity as to the ownership of shares in any national banking association is secured by a provision requiring that a list of the names and residences of all its shareholders, and the number of shares held by each, shall be kept in the office where its business is transacted, and shall, during business hours, be subject to the inspection of any shareholder or creditor of the association, and of the officers authorized to assess taxes under state authority. A copy of such list, verified by oath, must also be transmitted to the comptroller annually.

APPENDIX.

(20.) The national banks serve a very useful purpose, both to the government and the public, more especially in localities where there is not a sub-treasury, by acting, when so authorized by the secretary of the treasury, as depositories of public moneys and financial agents of the United States. For their services in this regard they receive no direct compensation, and are, moreover, required to give satisfactory security for the faithful performance of their duties and the safe custody and prompt payment of all public moneys intrusted to them, by a deposit with the treasurer of a sufficient amount of United States bonds.

(21.) The national banks are prohibited from loaning to any person, company, corporation, or firm, an amount exceeding one tenth part of their capital, and in estimating the liabilities of a company or firm the liabilities of its several members are to be included. They are thus, by law, made conservative in their management, and restrained from granting excessive loans, which would at least lessen their general usefulness to the communities in which they are situated and perhaps impair their safety.

(22.) They are further prohibited from making any loan or discount whatever on the security of the shares of their own capital stock, or from purchasing or holding the same unless to prevent loss upon a debt previously contracted in good faith. And, even in the latter case, they are not permitted permanently to hold or to cancel shares so obtained, but must, within six months from the date of their acquirement, sell or dispose of them at public or private sale.

(23.) They are also prohibited from becoming indebted or in any way liable to an amount exceeding that of their capital stock actually paid in, except on account (1) of their circulating notes; (2) their deposits or collections; (3) bills of exchange or drafts drawn against money actually on deposit to their credit or due to them; and (4) liabilities to their own stockholders for reserved profits. The purpose and effect of these provisions are to make the national banks lenders and not borrowers of money.

(24.) They are further forbidden, either directly or indirectly, to pledge or hypothecate any of their circulating notes for the purpose of procuring money with which to pay in or increase their capital stock, or for use in their banking operations, or otherwise. This restriction effectually precludes the practice, which was common in some former state systems, of employing the circulating notes of an association in the increase of its own capital, or in furnishing capital for a new association, which practice has at times been carried to an extreme limit.

(25.) The national banks are restricted in the rate of interest which they may take, receive, or reserve, to the rate allowed by the laws of the State, Territory, or District in which they are located.

(26.) A system of redemption of the circulating notes of the national banks is provided, whereby not only may they be readily converted into lawful money, but the mass of the circulation may be kept clean through the retirement of such portion as becomes worn or mutilated, and the issue of new notes by the comptroller, in their stead. This redemption is accomplished and compelled by requiring, first, that each national bank shall redeem its circulating notes at its own counter, at par, in lawful money on demand; second, that the notes of all closed banks shall be redeemed by the treasurer; third, that all worn, mutilated, or defaced national bank notes, which are received by any assistant treasurer or designated depository of the United States, shall be forwarded to the treasury for redemption; and, fourth, by providing that when the notes of any association, assorted or unassorted, are presented in sums of $1,000, or any multiple thereof, to the treasurer they shall be redeemed by that officer. The government is indemnified for all redemptions made by it, either by the bonds which it holds, as in the case of insolvent banks, or by a deposit of lawful money which is required to be previously made by all other banks.

(27.) If a national bank fails to pay its circulating notes, the comptroller is authorized to sell its bonds and provide for their payment. The government is indemnified against any possible loss from its guaranty of the payment of such circulating notes, by having reserved to it by law a paramount lien upon all the assets of any association which defaults in the redemption of its notes, to make good any deficiency arising from the sale of its bonds.

(28.) The destruction of all mutilated notes and of notes of closed banks, redeemed by the treasurer, is regulated by instructions of the secretary, given in pursuance of law. All notes destroyed are previously counted by separate agents or representatives of the secretary, the treasurer, the comptroller of the currency, and the banks which issued the notes; they are effectually mutilated by clipping and punching, to prevent their possible circulation should they by any remote chance pass out of the possession of the treasury before destruction; they are, in the presence of each of the agents mentioned, placed in a triple-locked macerating machine, where they are immediately ground into pulp; and their destruction is certified to by all the agents, both upon proper books in the treasury department and in certificates sent to the banks of issue.

(29.) The banks are prohibited, under a severe penalty, from certifying any check drawn upon them, unless the person or company drawing the check has at the time on deposit with them an amount of money equal to that specified in the check.

(30.) They are also prohibited from making any loan on the security of United States or national bank notes, or from agreeing for a consideration to withhold the same from use, the purpose of the prohibition being to prevent the "locking up" of money by the national banks, in the interests of speculators.

(31.) The officers of national banks are requried to make returns under oath to the treasurer of the United States and to pay to him in semi-annual installments an annual duty of one per cent. upon the average amount of their circulating notes, one half of one per cent. upon the average amount of their deposits, and a like rate upon the average amount of their capital stock beyond the amount invested in United States bonds. This duty is in lieu of all other *government taxes.*

(32.) The payment to the United States of the duties named does not, however, relieve the national banks from any liability to taxation by other than government authority, as it is expressly provided that nothing in the act shall prevent the shares of these associations from being taxed by the States as is other similar property, or shall exempt their real property from state, county, or municipal taxation, to the same extent as other real property.

(33.) Should the capital stock of any association become impaired in the course of business, by losses or otherwise, it must, within three months after the association shall have received notice from the comptroller, be made good by assessment upon the shareholders *pro rata* for the amount of stock held by them; and during such impairment the treasurer is required, upon notification from the comptroller, to withhold the interest on all bonds held by him in trust for such association. The authorized capital of the banks is thus by law compelled to be kept always intact, for the protection of their creditors.

(34.) When a national bank goes into voluntary liquidation, it must, within six months thereafter, deposit in the treasury an amount of lawful money equal to its entire outstanding circulation, which circulation is thereafter redeemed by the treasurer. Thus the banks, under existing law, derive no benefit from the accidental loss or destruction of any portion of their notes, such benefit inuring solely to the government.

(35.) Should any bank become insolvent, the most ample powers are possessed by the comptroller to take possession of such association, through a receiver to be appointed by him, and to proceed to collect its assets, and pay off, by dividends from time to time, the claims of its creditors. The note-holders are in such cases as secure as though the bank had remained solvent, the notes being protected by the bonds held by the government; while the other creditors have as a pro-

APPENDIX. 103

tection, in addition to the assets of the bank, the individual liability of the shareholders before mentioned, together with the capital paid in, no part of which can be returned to the shareholders until all approved claims against the association shall have been paid.

(36.) Mention has several times been made herein of the ample means provided in the National Bank Act for enforcing compliance with its provisions, by the infliction of penalties for their violation or non-observance. All of these penalties are severe, and many of them summary, the principal ones being here enumerated : —

I. For charging or exacting a usurious rate of interest, the whole interest agreed to be paid is forfeited; or, if actually paid, twice its amount may be recovered back by the person paying the same.

II. For certifying any check, unless the person by whom the check is drawn has on deposit with the association an amount of money equal to that represented by the check, the bank may be immediately closed by the appointment of a receiver.

III. For every day, after five days, in which a national bank shall fail to make and transmit to the comptroller any report of its condition called for by him, and for similar delay in transmitting to him the required proof of publication of such report, and also for every day, after ten days, in which a bank shall fail to transmit its semi-annual report of dividends and earnings, a penalty of one hundred dollars is imposed. And if any association fails or refuses to pay the amount of such penalty when assessed and demanded, the Treasurer of the United States is authorized to retain it, upon the order of the comptroller, out of the interest, as it may become due to the association, upon the bonds deposited to secure its circulation.

IV. For failure of the president or cashier of any association to report to the treasurer semi-annually, for purposes of taxation, the average amount of its notes in circulation, deposits, and capital stock not invested in United States bonds, a penalty of two hundred dollars is imposed, which may be collected as in the preceding paragraph. The treasurer may also, in such cases, assess the association upon the highest amount of its circulation, deposits, and capital stock, to be ascertained in such manner as he may deem best.

V. If an association fails to pay the duties assessed upon its circulation, deposits, and capital, such duties also may be reserved by the treasurer out of the interest falling due upon its bonds.

VI. The making of any loan upon the security of United States or national-bank notes, or agreeing for a consideration to withhold the same from use — in other words, the "locking up" of money, — is made a misdemeanor, punishable by a fine of one thousand dollars, and a further sum of one third of the money so loaned; and the officers making the loan are subject to the further penalty of one quarter of the money loaned.

VII. Embezzlement of the funds of an association by any of its officers, directors, or agents, or any false entry by any of them, in any book, statement, or report, with intent to injure or defraud the association or any other company or person, is punishable by imprisonment of not less than five nor more than ten years.

VIII. If any officer or agent of an association, whose charter has expired, knowingly reissues or puts into circulation any note, draft, check, or other security of such association, he is punishable by a fine of $10,000, or by imprisonment of from one to five years, or by both such fine and imprisonment.

IX. If the capital stock of any national bank falls below the minimum amount required by law, through the failure of any shareholder to pay the whole or any part of the amount of his subscription for such stock, and the deficiency in capital shall not be made good within thirty days thereafter, a receiver may be appointed to close up the affairs of the association.

X. Whenever the lawful money reserve of a national bank falls below the limit required by law, and remains below such limit for thirty days after receiving notice from the comptroller to make its reserve good, a receiver may be appointed and the bank closed.

XI. A receiver may also be appointed for any association which fails to redeem its circulating notes at its own counter or at the treasury, at par, on demand.

XII. If an association which accepts any shares of its own capital stock in order to prevent a loss upon a debt previously contracted in good faith (which is the only way in which such stock can be legally acquired by it), shall fail to sell such stock, at public or private sale, within six months thereafter, it may be closed by the appointment of a receiver.

XIII. Whenever an association fails to pay up its capital stock as required by law, or an impairment of its capital occurs by losses or otherwise, and it shall not, within three months after receiving notice from the comptroller, make good the deficiency by an assessment upon its shareholders, it may, unless it consents to go into liquidation, be placed in possession of a receiver and its business closed.

(37.) Finally, if the directors of any national banking association knowingly violate, or knowingly permit any of its officers, agents, or servants to violate *any* of the provisions of the National Bank Act, all the rights, privileges, and franchises of the association become thereby forfeited; in addition to which, every director who participates in or assents to such violation is held personally and individually responsible for all damages sustained by any person in consequence thereof.